The Writings on the Wall

RACHELLE PEART

CERINT MEDIA HOUSE

Unless otherwise indicated, all Scripture quotations are taken from the English Standard Version of the Bible.

First publication Copyright © 2017 by Rachelle Peart

THE WRITINGS ON THE WALL
by Rachelle Peart

Printed in United Kingdom

ISBN 978-0-9956796-5-8

Write to:
Rachelle Peart
4 Telford Street
Northampton NN5 4EU
Phone No: 07961760168
E-mail: info@chayelle.com

All rights reserved.
No part of this publication may be reproduced, stored in a retrieval system or transmitted in any form or by any means, electronic, mechanical, photocopying, recording or otherwise without prior permission of the publisher.

Cerint Media House
www.cerintmedia.com
+44(0)7502373695

Contents

Dedication... vi
Acknowledgement... vii
Foreword... xi

PART ONE
God speaking and speaking to God

Love Letter..3
The circle of happiness................................10
But 13
God's transforming process..........................15
Just pray..17
The sacrificial lamb.....................................19

PART TWO
Godly women

Woman of faith..23
Woman of strength 25
Mothers..27
Who am I: I am mother 28
You are..30
A purpose driven life...................................31

PART THREE
Prose: Pages on

Caring 37
Loving yourself 38
Moving on 40
Sharing a problem 41
Friends 42
Changes 44

PART FOUR
Thus says the Lord

Thus says the Lord 47
Life is real 48
My navigation my guide 50
Rooted & grounded 51
The Master's love 52
What You see 53
Today I feel 54
Christ is qualified 56

PART FIVE
The fruit of the Spirit

Faithfulness 61
Joy 62

Love..63
Patience..64
Peace..65
Kindness...67
Self-control..68
Goodness...69
Gentleness...70

PART SIX
Flow

A virgin's tale...73
The earth is the Lord's...................................76
When music speaks.......................................78
The colour of my emotions............................80

POSTSCRIPT

Much to do about nothing..............................83
You have my heart...85
Falling in love with Jesus..............................86

Glossary 87

DEDICATION

I dedicate this book to my husband Bryan Peart and my sons Caiyan Peart and Hezekiah Malachi Peart (now sleeping with the angels). I love you and thank you for your love and support over the years. God is great and He made a way for us, so I just want to give Him thanks for His goodness.

I also want to make special mention of my spiritual mother Rev Earla Green (sorry Mum). I don't know if I'd be standing today without your prayers and encouragement. You have spoken so many prophetic words over my life. You have displayed so much wisdom in helping me deal with my life's struggles. Never would have made it without you. Thank you so much for embracing me so lovingly. Now the eagle has left its nest! (Big smile)

ACKNOWLEDGEMENTS

My Lord, my Saviour, my Redeemer. Lord, I just want to express my thanks and gratitude for loving me unconditionally. For having faith in me, for forgiving me and for never giving up on me. Without you, nothing is possible but with you all things are possible.

You are my strength and I will be eternally indebted to you. Only your grace and mercy have brought me through some of the darkest times of my life. You love like no other and when my back was against the wall you kept me going. In good times, laughter, joy or pain. You gave me beauty for ashes and the oil of joy for my pain.

Because of you, I was able to put away my sackcloth and pick myself up. There is no other God like you and I am a testament to Your greatness. I thank You for the Holy Spirit operating in my life because, without it, life would be insignificant. Lord, I just want to say I love You and thank You for bringing me thus far.

I would like to thank my mother Marjorie Brown for raising such a determined, high-spirited daughter. You have loved me in all the ways you could. You have been there consistently when I have needed you.

Thank you for providing for me and I appreciate you and love you. Also thanks to my extended family.

To my prayer partner Trecia Smith, many prayers have been answered over the phone on a Wednesday morning. God is good and I thank you for reminding me at times when my flesh had wanted to take over, the power and effectiveness of fervent prayer. We have seen many results!

To my dear sister Santana Morris. Thanks for praying with me and transcending time zones and thanks for encouraging me.

Janine Clarke, my editor and fellow prayer partner. Thanks for taking on the mundane task of making sure this book was print ready. God bless you.

To my prayer warriors on the WhatsApp group; birthed out of a week of fasting - God is great! We are still going strong. Thank you for all the prayers and support the encouragement and the love. Thank you for all the emergency prayers, the early morning prayers and the late night ones. Keep praying as prayer changes things and things change when we pray.

To my WEC ladies; you are truly an inspiration. You have shown me the results of what happens when ladies come together empowered by the love of God. Thank you for accepting the baby. It is amazing how God puts people together at pivotal points in their lives; how He just aligns and orchestrates it is mind blowing!

Thanking all my cheerleaders Marsha Morgan, Joy Adams, Janine Clarke, Marie Warrington, Jennifer and Donville Davis, Nadine Forde, Mrs C, Issachar Green, Samantha Green, Darren Evans-Henry, Yvonne Allen and Aunty Belzie. For your love, kind words and support over the years. I couldn't have done it without you all. Darren you have been inquiring about the release of my book for a very long time; so here it is now. You have also provided a platform for me to minister in poetry and spoken words.

An immense 'Thank you' to my church family at COP - I truly love you all dearly. You have supported me in so many ways. I have grown into the woman of God I am today because of the church.

I want to say a big thank you to Bishop Burrell and Sis B for providing opportunities for me to grow in my faith. God bless you both.

A very special heart warming thanks to my publishers at Cerint Media House. Lauretta Amata Olowu I pray God with bless you bountifully for tarrying with a novice author like myself. You stuck with me through all the changes and created this gem. I am really proud of your work. Thank you for making my dream a reality.

A heart felt thank you to my new church family at College Street, Northampton NTCG. Pastor Donovan Allen and team you have made my family and I feel truly welcome and at home in this new environment. God bless you all.

Thanks to all my family, friends and well wishers who have supported me in any way shape or form over the years. Your kindness has not gone amiss. I give thanks for those who have prayed for me or with me, encouraged me, laughed or cried with me. I pray God's blessings over your lives.

Love Rachelle

FOREWORD

I am extremely thankful and excited to be able to present and publish this book of poetry. From a very young age, I was drawn to writing poetry. One of my earliest memories of writing poems was while I was in year 3 at Primary School. Ever since then, my love of poetry has continued to grow.

I remember writing poems to help me get through different seasons of life. When I gave my heart to Christ, my style of writing changed suddenly. The things I wrote in the preceding years now been revamped to suit a more Christian living style of writing.

It's amazing how when you quieten your heart towards God, He can download words to you which become poems. The bible says in Luke 6:45b "for of the abundance of his heart his mouth speaks. Whatever is inside will come out by some means and if it is not expressed verbally, then poetry speaks about what is inside the heart".

I have a deep passion for writing and even a deeper passion in sharing information that will edify and build up others.

I have written these poems over the years on and off. When I write, it is by the inspiration of God and it flows naturally.

But I've come to realise the gift lays dormant if it is not used until you put yourself in a position to exercise the gift. That could be a moment of reflection, reading, meditating and quieting your heart before God. I am so thrilled to finally be able to officially say I am an author. To God be the glory, great things He has done! Look what the Lord has done. If He did it for me, He will do it for you! There is a writer in you.

PART ONE

God speaking and speaking to God

LOVE LETTER

So I thought I'd write you a love letter
To let you know how I feel
Of how these feelings I have for you,
Truly are real
At first, I tried to deny it,
Then tried to hide it
I put off my desires
For things that had more appeal
But in the end
I couldn't put my feelings for you
Aside any longer
Let me take you on my love journey...

Dear JC,

It's been a while since I had a heart-to-heart with you. When I first got to know you, I didn't know what I was getting into. I was young, naïve even a bit immature. I didn't take your word lightly, but I also didn't know what I was signing up to.

As the years pass and our relationship matured, I reached the level where I was getting a bit close to you. And I know for sure if my circumstances didn't change when it did, I would have carried on getting closer to you.

When I changed my address, it was not my wish to try and avoid you, even though in retrospect it could easily feel this way. Still you never left me; you were still by my side.

I carried on in the relationship but there was not much fuel to my fire. It became complacency and I did 'us' because that's what I had become accustomed to doing, and deep down I knew you were good for me. I didn't know any other like you at the time and it just felt right being with you.

But throughout this, I was cheating on you with 'human'. I thought about you but I was also thinking of another. I came home on Sundays but failed to develop an intimate relationship with you throughout the rest of the week. It's almost like I forgot about you when I left the house and when I would return I would pick up where I left off. But you were not happy; I could tell because this was driving a wedge between us.

We were drifting apart as our meeting became fewer and more far between. I came home less and less as my circumstances meant I had to work on days I was supposed to be coming home to you. I suddenly had to prioritise and you were not on the top of my list even though, I wanted you to be. In hindsight when I had a free day or two, I could have made more of an effort to see you and develop our relationship within the privacy of our home.

I felt bad at times for leading you on, for teasing you but not having full contact with you. However, there was a pull, this inert feeling that I would get now and then; it was a real tug of war. On the days I had was to go to work; the days I should be spending with you, I often would think that if only I didn't have to work then I would certainly dedicate this time to be with you.

But then, even when this wish was finally granted, I came to you but someone else had occupancy and had taken up residence. I was battling with my feelings for him for a long time and I didn't know how to let it go.

I sought to please others before considering your needs, not knowing you needed me more than they ever did, and for that I'm sorry. But I know you have forgiven me for that because it's not like you to hold grudges right?

Eventually, a friend turned to me one day and excitedly proclaimed she was so in love and she wanted to share with me the 'love manual'. Yeah, a love manual you know! Sounds crazy seeing as being with you so long, you would have thought I would have known how to love and care for you by now.

I couldn't get mad, knowing that all my life I have had you, but I didn't know you like I should. She said I needed to commit myself fully and wholeheartedly to you and no one else, and then you would give me all I could ever want and need in return.

She told me that you would give me your debit card to withdraw when I was running low. That you would deposit into my account and all my cares and worries I could cast on you. Whenever you made a date with me, you would certainly show up she told me and you would never cancel my appointments in your diary.

And so there it was, I started feeling you getting close to me and I was loving it. I loved loving and being loved back. It started to feel real. But still, I had strong feelings for this other one I had grown strong affection for, so my heart was in one place and my head in another.

But I had hopes and I felt it very soon after coming in contact with you on a personal level that I couldn't carry on having a somewhat mediocre relationship with you. You raised the bar higher and you challenged me.

And if you know me very well, you will know that I'm a girl who loves challenges, so I said to myself "you just wait and see". I was dead set. I was going to prove my love for you and I wanted to declare it so all could know. So boldly I decided "This is it!" like Michael Jackson said.

This time I was going to say the guy is mine. I wanted what everybody else had with you. I wanted to feel you near me; I wanted you to talk to me; to whisper sweet words of comfort. I wanted to trust you because everyone knows the foundation of any good relationship is trust. I wanted to be passionate about you and to proclaim to everyone I came in contact with who my man was.

I knew you had a purpose for being in my life and the plans you had for me. You wanted to go to bed with me; you wanted me to be the first person you saw when I woke up in the mornings. The one I would travel with on a daily basis to and from work.

At work, you wanted to be on my mind amongst my busy schedule. When things went wrong you wanted to be the first person I would call on. When I lacked anything, you were ever so kind towards me.

You wanted to buy me the nicest clothes, put food in my fridge, buy me that dream car and that dream house. You wanted to set up that business for me and take me on long cruises across the transatlantic.

You always told me that you were there for me. All I had to do was reach out and you would put aside everything, at the drop of a hat, just to be with me. When everything else around me was crumbling, you were the only one that remained constant throughout.

It took me to pursue someone else and had it not been for him breaking my heart, I wouldn't see the good man I had right there in front of me, while I was going around trying to find an incompatible match.

And so you gave me the ultimatum to come back to you to continue what we started so long ago, you told me not to resist anymore and then you showed me what staying out of love with you had cost. I say to you that it wasn't worth it all.

So, I left myself open to all these plans you had for my life, I wanted them and I wanted them badly.

There I was flat on my back, I never dreamed this could happen to me, it felt so good, it felt so real! I was in love with you, you were in love with me and I had come back to you. It was a wonderful experience and after we made that contact I knew things would never be the same again.

I was happy and I was rejoicing. I longed for this unknowingly for so long and there it was. Then you didn't stop there, you elevated me even further and just like McDonalds 'I'm loving it'.

For the first time in my life, I can truly say I really do love you and there's no other like you. It is you I desire and it took me all this time to find this out. I have fallen in love with you deeply and I look forward to spending the rest of my life in perfect union, in one accord with you.

I am thankful for all the things I went through, because if I didn't go through what I went through, I wouldn't know you like I do. I love you and I will never let you down. Love forever and always.

Your girl,
RAM

THE CIRCLE OF HAPPINESS

Being happy involves being satisfied
With the four elements of your life:
Emotional,
Physical,
Financial
And
Spiritual.
These are four integral parts
In the circle of happiness.

FINANCIAL
Having enough money
where you don't have to watch
The pennies as you spend.
But this is only one element
And does not guarantee happiness.
Everyone knows
Money alone
Doesn't make you happy.

PHYSICAL
Being physically well
Does add a quarter
In the circle of happiness.
It's very obvious that if you can run,
Jump and skip about without difficulty
Then you are happier than someone
Who has had that taken away

Whether from birth,
Accidentally
Or by lifestyle choices.

EMOTIONAL
The third piece to the puzzle is
Emotional happiness;
it's the one that's most compelling.
A lot of people struggle with it
Because it might be the most
Fundamental key to your happiness.

SPIRITUAL
The final element is played
Down as not valued
By a lot of people as being important.
Once you can find inner peace,
Serenity, love and joy
Then it all becomes clear.
Spiritual happiness comes
From having that deep
And personal relationship with God.
So much so that you can relax
In His presence
And trust God to be your all in all.

Most people throughout their lives
Find elements of happiness.

If you're lucky you might achieve
Two or three elements,
But only a few people develop all four.
Then and only then will you've completed
A full cycle in the circle of happiness.

Scripture Reference:
Delight yourself in the Lord, and he will give you the desires of your heart.
Psalm 37:4

BUT

But I am tired and have no strength...
 "I'll lift you up on wings like an eagle,"
  He said.
But I have no hope...
 "Have faith,"
  He said.
But I have no future...
 "For I know the plans I have for you,"
  He said.
But I am anxious...
 "Be anxious for nothing, but in everything
  by prayer and supplication,"
   He said.
But I feel so sad...
 "I will give you joy, overflowing like rivers,"
  He said.
But I am hungry...
 "I will give you the bread of life and you
  shall be filled,"
   He said.
But I am thirsty...
 "Just drink of my water, you will neve
  thirst again,"
   He said.
But I am still so young...
 "Remember now thy creator in the days of
  thy youth",
   He said.

But I am troubled...
> *"When troubles all around never gonna leave you, don't let it get you down, I won't forsake you,"*
> He said.

But I have nothing to wear...
> *"Render your heart not the garment,"*
> He said.

But I can't...
> *"You can do all things through Christ who strengthens you,"*
> He said

This man always knows
The right thing to say.
The way he speaks
Puts me at ease.
I can meditate on the words
And find truth in it.
It's a beautiful thing.
Oh, I love him!

Scripture Reference:
Your word is a lamp for my feet, a light on my path.
Psalm 119:105 (NIV)

GOD'S TRANSFORMATION PROCESS

Like olive
Being pressed into oil

Like gold
Being refined
So the Lord our God presses to purify us

Like bronze
Expanding before it sets
So the Lord our God stretches us
To fill in the finest details

Like silver,
He separates us from others
So He can see us in our purest forms

Like grapes
Being produced into wine
So He extracts all that goodness within us
To make the finest and most tasteful

Like carbon
Being pressed into diamond
So He applies intense pressure
To make us rise

Like a volcano
Making the most beautiful
And unbreakable gem of character

You see our most valuable parts of our beings
have been through a process.
Our Spirit has been refined
by the blood of Jesus.
This is God working in and through us.
A Work in Progress (WIP);
He is creating and moulding us
to be the very best.

Christ is the master of His trade.
He takes the time to perfect us
In his pureness, holiness
And righteousness.
Wait on the Lord
As He refines you.
The best is yet to come.

Do not halt the process
Before the work has been completed.
You will miss the treasure at the end.
Be encouraged
And be strong in the Lord.
Pray for my strength
And pray for me
While I pray for you.
God bless you all

Scripture Reference:
Psalm 12:6, Numbers 31:23, Malachi 3:3

JUST PRAY

When it's too overwhelming to grasp,
   JUST PRAY
When you're too sad to confide in someone,
   JUST PRAY
When you are so happy and you can't gather you thoughts,
   JUST PRAY
When you are too angry to stay focus,
   JUST PRAY
When your mood gets seasonal and changes like the English weather,
   JUST PRAY
When you need to reach down and find that extra drive to motivate yourself,
   JUST PRAY
When troubles all around,
   JUST PRAY
When stress gets a hold of you,
   JUST PRAY
When there's no one around,
   JUST PRAY
Depression
   JUST PRAY
Happy times
   JUST PRAY
Marital problems
   JUST PRAY
Tiredness
   JUST PRAY

Brokenness
    JUST PRAY

Even when you don't feel like it
    JUST GET DOWN ON YOUR KNEES
        AND JUST PRAY!
I've found the remedy to all of life's problems
    Is to...
    JUST PRAY.
Pour your heart out to your father.
    All your needs he will supply if you
    JUST PRAY.
No matter what the seasons or the reason
    Don't forget to
    JUST PRAY.
Thank you Lord Jesus for the opportunity to
    JUST PRAY!

        Scripture Reference:
        Pray without ceasing
        1 Thessalonian 5:17 (KJV)

THE SACRIFICIAL LAMB

I am the lamb who was slain,
I was offered as a sacrifice
Your salvation I came to claim
Ram is my name
But look at me
Pitiful me
To be offered up as a living sacrifice?

Look at my eyes
They disguise
Look at my tongue
They do not tell lies
Why choose me, the lamb
Out of all the other animals
To signify redeeming my companions to God
The perfect sacrificial offering
By my blood
I'll tell you why

I am a symbol of gentleness of character
and patience
under suffering
I signify purity, meekness and sacrifice

I am borne as a symbol of Christ
I am the emblem of faith

I am the holy lamb; granted to a brave,
resolute spirit, who would even undertake
war for Christ's cause
Worthy is the lamb
Worthy I am
The precious lamb of God

Worthy to take the scroll and break its seal
I am me,
I am the RAM
I am Christ who died to save all from sin
Behold the Lamb of God who takes away
the sin of the world

Scripture Reference:
Revelation 5

PART TWO

Godly Women

WOMAN OF FAITH

You are beautiful;
your heart is beautiful beyond compare
You are radiant;
God's love shines in your heart
You are a virtuous woman of God
A Chayil: a perfect wife,
The ideal woman
You are a woman of self- worth
You are the personification of wisdom
So powerful,
Yet so humble,
Loving and true to God's word
We salute you
Purpose woman of God

You are kind;
a woman of good character,
your worth is far more
Than rubies, gold and fine silver
You are wise;
you have wisdom,
Knowledge and understanding
You never burn out
Your door is always open:
 welcoming and inviting

You sing with a voice
So heavenly and angelic
You gird yourself with strength
You dress divinely;
Strength and honour
Are your clothing
You are fearfully
And wonderfully made
Charm is deceitful
And beauty is passing
But a woman who fears the Lord,
She shall be praised.

Scripture Reference:
Proverbs 31

WOMAN OF STRENGTH

Strength and vigour are yours to hold
Many stories you've been told
Yet still your ear listens relentlessly
You are divine
You are one of a kind
A great leader
A Deborah

Your wisdom encourages
You are a Mother
A mentor
A Counsellor
A mighty warrior for Christ
A commander chief
You are courageous
On the battlefield constantly
You do not falter
You do not faint

Subtly you drop a hint of radiance
You're beautiful inside and out
The grace of God shines in
 and through you

Age is your strategy
And experience is your instrument
To win souls for Christ
You are a great teacher

A master of your trade
Yet a heart so soft and tender
And a sense of humour you sport

The eyes of the Lord are upon you
He has blessed you,
With knowledge, understanding
And a discerning spirit
Your faith in God is your weapon
A passionate and righteous witness for Christ
We salute you as a sensational woman of God

Scripture Reference:
Judges 4

MOTHERS

We are teachers
We are nurses
We are doctors

We are mechanics
We are ministers
We are counsellors

We are psychologist
We are bosses
We are leaders

We are comedians
We are accountants
We are auditors

We are bankers
We are actors
We are entertainers

We are stewards
We are disciples
We are Chayils

Scripture Reference:
Her children rise up and call her blessed:
Proverbs 31:28a (NKJV)

WHO I AM: MOTHER

I am a nurse;
    I comfort you when you're sick
I am a clown;
    I keep you smiling

I am a lawyer;
    I argue your case
I am a nurturer;
    I take good care of you

I am a manager;
    I sort out the day to day running of your life
I am a teacher;
    I guide you

I am a nutritionist;
    I keep you healthy
I am a cleaner;
    I mop up your mess

I am a cook;
    I make sure you eat delicious meals
I am a fashion guru;
    I fix you up real nice

I am a launderer;
    I keep your clothes clean

I am a mentor;
    I stare you in the right direction
I am your friend, confidant, your team
    leader, your sergeant, your support.

I am your spiritual coach;
    I point you to Christ
I am here even when you don't need me.
    I am your life, your heart, most of all,

I am your mother
    God made me a steward
        Over your life.

Scripture Reference:
Behold, children are a heritage from the Lord, the fruit of the womb a reward.
Psalm 127:3

YOU ARE...

You are my life
You are my soul

You are my truth
You are my love

You are my joy
You are my peace

You are my God
You are my way

You are my light
You are strength

You are my rock
You are my source

You are my shield
You are my hope

You are everything
You are my God

Scripture Reference:
I am the vine; you are the branches. Whoever abides in me and I in him, he it is that bears much fruit, for apart from me you can do nothing.
John 15:5

A PURPOSE-DRIVEN LIFE

On a mission,
Lord, tell me what is my purpose?
I want to find out before the minister says
    ashes to ashes and dust to dust
Don't want to go to my grave
Having been a slave
To my unrealised hopes and dreams
Of reaching people, changing lives and
    advancing the kingdom of God
I don't want to aid the graveyard
And help it be rich
With unused gifts and talents
I want to unlock my greatest potential
    before I die
And if He should take me
Before my work on earth is done
I would die an unhappy one
I promise to walk in the purpose God
    ordained for me
I want to spread the gospel
    so the blind can see
I will be the light and the salt
Before my days on earth draws to a halt
I know that it starts with God
I wasn't an accident
I need to consider what drives my life
I was made to last forever
    but not in this realm

If I look at things through God's glasses,
I would see things from his point of view
Life is only a temporary assignment
That's why it's crucial that you make your
purpose the reason for everything
the reason you eat, sleep, talk, learn,
watch and grow

I was planned for God's pleasure,
so therefore
I need to consider what makes God smile
I need to come back to the heart of worship,
where it's all about Him
I need to be God's friend, in fact, His best friend
So therefore I need to develop a relationship with him
Even when he seems distant

I was created to be part of His family
What matters most?
You know that's love, a place to belong and experience life together
We need to cultivate a community spirit amongst us,
Whilst restoring broken fellowship and protecting our church.

I was created to become like Christ
Learning to grow in Him and let Him
   transform me by the truth of His word,
Through the troubles I face,
I know I grow through temptation,
So I count it all joy when I face adversities
   Because I know, it takes time.

I must accept my assignment,
I was shaped for serving God
I need to understand my shape
That is my
   SPIRITUAL GIFTS,
      HEART,
         ABILITIES,
            PERSONALITY AND
            EXPERIENCES.

I need to use what God gave me
Enlighten me dear Lord
   On how real servants act,
Because I know I was created
To SERVE and to GIVE
I need to meditate on Gods power in my
   weakness
As His grace is sufficient for me
   because
      His strength is perfected in my
      weakness

I was made for a mission
I must share my life message
That will enable me to become a World-
 Class Christian
The one who has balance in her life
Because I have lived a life of Purpose.

Inspired by A Purpose Driven Life by Rick Warren

Scripture Reference:
For I know the plans I have for you, declares the Lord, plans for welfare and not for evil, to give you a future and a hope
Jeremiah 29:11

PART THREE

Prose: Pages on...

CARING

Who cares enough?
Who will be there when times get tough?
Who will be there in my hour of need?
Who will be there to hold my hand?
Who will care and understand?

Will there be tears of joy?
Or will there be laughter?
As I walk this lonely route
Who will be there to care?
Share, endure and secure it with me
Jesus Christ is the answer

He is there
He is dear
A very present help in times of trouble
He knows
He understands
He cares

Scripture Reference:
God is our refuge and strength, a very present help in trouble
Psalm 46:1

LOVING YOURSELF

Love yourself before you find the route
to loving anyone else.
Unconditional and unedifying love.
I have to love myself
And be happy within myself
before the love and joy brings out
the happiness I have inside.

If you search for a human being to love you
as much as you want to be loved,
You'll probably never find it
in your lifetime
But if you set the guidelines for loving
yourself as much as Christ loves you,
You'll reach your target for love.

Know that Jesus loves you much more than
you could ever imagine.
When you learn to love yourself you can
understand and love God with all your
heart.
It's that agape love.

It's the kind of love you'll find from no one else,
Only He knows how to love you,
Only He knows how to care for you,
Your innermost being he knows,
Your thoughts and desires.

Scripture Reference:
We love because he first loved us.
1 John 4:19

MOVING ON

Christ is the controller of the decisions in your life.
He decides when it's the right time to move on and pack it in.
No point in sitting there waiting for that great change to come,
when you know it is not going to happen.

Whether it's a bad relationship, your living arrangements, your job, your business or a hobby.
God decides when these things aren't right for you,
Closes the door and tells you to move on.
When that time comes,
    move on.
When God gets ready, you have to move.
The bible says
    Faith without works is dead.

Scripture Reference:
Forget what happened in the past, and do not dwell on events from long ago.
Isaiah 43:18 (GW)

SHARING A PROBLEM

I've heard many times
    A problem shared is a problem halved.
Well sharing your issues with your Lord
    it helps a lot.
He is willing to hear you out
    And will never cancel your appointment
        in his diary.
You may feel embarrassed at first
    Or fed up because you feel like you are
        always complaining,
But keeping it to yourself
    Will kill you inside and it hurts even longer.
A bit of good encouragement
    From a caring individual never goes amiss
And never fails to help the healing process.
    You may also feel
You don't want your emotions to let loose
    But a good cry also helps.
There are always enough tears
    For every problem
And don't feel like you shouldn't
    Or it's out of place for you to cry.

Scripture Reference:
We know that all things work together for the good of those who love God: those who are called according to His purpose.
Romans 8:28 (HCSC)

GOD-FEARING FRIENDS

It's true when they say that true ones
are precious and rare,
you try to study even the ones you thought
were true
and contemplate whether or not they are
truly classified friend.

It's when we go through life's changes that
we figure out if we have friends.
If you come out on the other side with the
person still by your arm then you know.
If majors things happening your life or
there's and you still end up
by each other's side as if nothing
then you know you have real friends.

Like a relationship with a man/woman,
a friendship will never be totally and
exclusively complete.

You'll find qualities/traits in one that you
fail to find in the other.
The key is not letting it bother you or else
you'll end up missing out on the other
things they are good at.
The relationship must also be maintained
by both parties or the interest will die.
It needs communication to flourish.

The qualities I look for is someone who cares,
that is there to be called upon who shares your joy, grief and other emotions,
someone you could approach and talk to,
someone who is kind and willing to go the extra mile for you,
somewhere an ordinary person wouldn't go.
Someone who is God-fearing.
Now if my friends have not got all or most of these traits then you're not really my true friend. Are you?

Oh and don't forget to be understanding and be there ready to listen when I need you to.
Then again I myself must be willing to be all that and more to someone I classify as a friend.
Friendless? Jesus is the only friend everyone truly needs.
Seek Him out today, He is ready, willing able and available.

Scripture Reference:
A man of many companions may come to ruin, but there is a friend who sticks closer than a brother.
Proverbs 18:24

CHANGES

My mind is ruptured with thoughts and feelings.
It's a constant battlefield being created
storing some wild random views.
The woman in me thinks too much
but with time on your hands to think,
what else to do?

My feelings are simple
yet quite complex in its development.
It's always why or why not.
Trying constantly
to figure out solutions and remedies
to problems
Going through changes
I can't even understand.
But going to God
He understands
He will figure it out

Scripture Reference:
Jesus Christ is the same yesterday and today and forever.
Hebrews 13:8

PART FOUR

Thus says the Lord

THUS SAYS THE LORD

With me by your side,
you have nothing to worry about.
If you worry
it's because you choose to
I am always feeling what you're feeling
getting emotionally involved
and worrying for you.
When you're sad,
I'm sadder
When you're happy,
I am even happier.
You don't know how much your emotions
are mutually connected to mine
and it's not a mind over matter thing.
I can't separate the two.
We are one at least in my eyes.
I share your emotions.

Scripture Reference:
Be strong and courageous. Do not be afraid or terrified because of them, for the LORD your God goes with you; he will never leave you nor forsake you.
Deuteronomy 31:6 (NIV)

LIFE IS REAL:
A CONFESSION FROM THE HEART

Real peace starts
With putting your mind at rest,
At ease with the trials and tribulations
You are facing
And resting in the arms of our Lord.

Real love starts
When you push that release button
That tells your heart to go
And fall in love with Jesus.
And if you slip up,
Real love says
He keep on loving and forgiving.

Real passion starts
When you find you can't live
Without Christ in your life

Real kindness begins
When you are willing to sacrifice
Just to see someone with real happiness.

Real sacrifice says
It was the hardest thing
I have ever had to do
But my motivation remains in the report.
This makes my heart yearn,
So I won't give up now.

Real struggle comes about
When life is not so easy
And you are barely making it through.
But with Jehovah Jireh by our side,
We've just got to give thanks in advance.

Real praise and adoration reflects
Good spirit, true worthiness and gratitude.

Real people possess
The overall life skills and qualification
Of appreciating life, others
And living to build the kingdom of heaven.

Real people show
Real praise and adoration
For our Father who helped them
Through real struggle
And made real sacrifice for them.
They return the favour with real kindness,
Real passion and real love for him.
This brings about real peace and joy
In our daily lives. Life is real

Scripture Reference
Jesus Christ is the same yesterday and today and forever.
Hebrews 13:8

MY NAVIGATION; MY GUIDE

You tell me where to go
You provide JEHOVAH JIREH
You steer me in the right direction
To help me to not make a wrong selection
You tell me to turn left,
turn right.
You warn me when there are speed bumps ahead
and tell me to slow down
When I reach a roundabout,
you tell me to keep my eyes straight ahead.
Around the corners of life,
you curb me
And when I am on the straight and narrow,
you tell me not to become complacent;
but to keep watch
because somewhere along the road,
something will come up trying to catch me out.
You warn me of dangers and hazards ahead.
You bring me through the best route.
When I've gone in a different direction,
you have helped me to re-route

Scripture Reference:
Your word is a lamp to my feet and a light to my path.
Psalm 119:105

ROOTED AND GROUNDED

Rooted and grounded
Firm and deep
In the bosom of my Saviour's arms
I safely sleep
Rooted and grounded in his love
His love is not partial
It's sent from above

Rooted and grounded
ever so strong
He's there for me
whether I'm right or wrong

Rooted and grounded
Though tossed by the wind
His peace he gives;
it keeps me still

Rooted and grounded
in my faith
My anchor holds
In my Saviour's love

Scripture Reference:
Rooted and built up in Him and established in the faith, as you have been taught, abounding in it with thanksgiving.
Colossians 2:7 (NKJV)

THE MASTER'S LOVE

It's love that can't be measured
Can't be quantified
But the quality of this love
will last forever

It can't be poured out
It's that warm embrace
It's that sweet kiss
It's the love that doesn't
cost a thing

There's no limit to my love
My love,
I give you freely
Freely as I give,
take my love.

Scripture Reference:
Greater love has no one than this, that someone lay down his life for his friends.
John 15:13

WHAT YOU SEE

You look at me without judgment
I see brokenness, you see treasure
I feel hurt and pain, you see pleasure
I see failure and disappointment;
you see your desire in me
Lord make me and mold me into the person
you want me to be
I see filthy rags
You see a vessel ready to be used by you
I see anger,
you see righteousness and holiness
I see the curse of strongholds and soul ties,
But you see liberty and joy

You see when we look at things
through the naked fleshly eye,
we see it all wrong.
You have to take on the mind of Christ
and look at yourself spiritually
through the eyes of Truth.
Deception dare not come near.
I see myself as Christ sees me...

Scripture Reference:
For as the heavens are higher than the earth,
so are my ways higher than your ways and my
thoughts than your thoughts.
Isaiah 55:9

TODAY I FEEL:

Blessed as Jabez
Fearful as Paul
Magnificent as Moses

Wonderful as Noah
Favoured as Joseph
Strong as Samson

Powerful as Joshua
Loving as Jesus
Faithful as Abraham

As kind as the good Samaritan
As patient as Job
As obedient as Samuel

As prayerful as Daniel
As humble as Mary
As virtuous as the Proverbs 31 woman

As wise as Solomon
As purposeful as Esther
As bold as Peter

As soulful as David
As energetic as James
As brave as Rahab

There are times in life
when you're going through.
A burden so heavy
You can't see your way through
Call on the Father
that's all you have to do
Then seal it
by praising your way through

The value of learning
from your mistakes
Stops you going through
that deadly repetitive cycle
Every lesson learned
helps build your character

Scripture Reference:
Not only so, but we also glory in our sufferings,
because we know that suffering produces persever-
ance; perseverance, character; and character, hope.
Romans 5:3-4 (NIV)

CHRIST IS QUALIFIED

If God was a doctor,
He would have all the remedies
If God was a nurse,
He would monitor you around the clock
If God was a counsellor,
He would offer sound advice
If God was a teacher,
He would teach you what you need to know

If God was a lawyer,
He would argue your case
If God was a Judge,
He would be the fairest
If God was an accountant,
He would keep the most accurate financial records
If God was a mentor,
He would produce the best protégés

If God was a soldier,
He would fight the good fight
If God was an architect,
He would draw the best designs
If God was a scientist,
He would discover the best inventions
If God was a bus driver,
He would take you to your destination right on time

If God was a pastor,
He would preach the best sermons
If God was a cleaner,
He would make the place spotless
If God was a comedian,
He would tell the best jokes
If God was an actor,
He would put on the best show

You see,
God is qualified for every job role.
There is no job too small
or too large for Him.
Why don't you trust him today
to control every part of your life?

(Because He is qualified)

Scripture Reference:
I will instruct you and teach you in the way you should go; I will counsel you with my eye upon you.
Psalm 32:8

PART FIVE

The fruit of the Spirit; the Characteristics of a true Christian

FAITHFULNESS

Faithfulness is righteousness
Faithfulness is endurance

Faithfulness is loyalty
Faithfulness is trustworthiness

Faithfulness is provision
Faithfulness is merciful

Faithfulness is abiding
Faithfulness is truthfulness

Faithfulness is merciful
Faithfulness is certainty

Faithfulness is accurate

Scripture Reference:
2 Corinthians 5:7
Luke 16:10-12
1 John 1:9
1 Corinthians 10:13
Psalm 91:4
2 Timothy 2:13
Jeremiah 29:11
Proverbs 20:6

JOY

Joy is delight
Joy is hope

Joy is humility
Joy is pleasure

Joy is sharing
Joy is rejoicing

Joy is peace
Joy is happiness

Joy is mirth
Joy is enjoying

Joy is confidence
Joy is comfort

Joy is gladness
Joy is sowing
Joy is contentment

Scripture References:
The joy of the Lord is your strength
Nehemiah 8:10b
Pslam 16:11
Psalm 126:5

LOVE

Love is kindness
Love is flowing
Love is forgiveness
Love is tolerance
Love is united

Love is passion
Love is caring
Love is honest
Love is goodness
Love is acceptance

Love is endurance
Love is trust
Love is calm
Love is compassion
Love is grace

Love is respect
Love is empathetic
Love is source
Love is longsuffering
Love is conquering

Scripture References:
1 John 4:7-8; 1 Corinthians 13:4-7
Deuteronomy 6:5; John 3:16
Mark 12:30-31; Proverbs 10:12

PATIENCE

Patience is tolerance
Patience is longsuffering
Patience is trust
Patience is endurance
Patience is waiting
Patience is faith
Patience is testing
Patience is perseverance

Patience is rest
Patience is character building
Patience is having confidence
Patience is hope
Patience is strength
Patience is refining
Patience is renewing
Patience is deliverance

It is described as the power or capacity to endure without complaint something difficult or disagreeable, forbearance, longsuffering.

Scripture References:
1 John 5:14
Psalm 37:7
Romans 5:4
Isaiah 40:31.

PEACE

Peace is when we lie down
in green pastures
Peace is when we rest
in God's bosom
Peace is your soul panting
for water
Peace is the freedom
from all disturbances of this world

Peace is relaxing and throwing down
all the weight;
leaving it on God's to-do list
Peace is letting go
and letting God
Peace is trusting in Jesus Christ
to be all He promised to be

Perfect peace is a slice of heaven
Peace is God's perfect timing

Peace is quietness
Peace is stillness
Peace is calmness

Peace is serenity
Peace is tranquillity
Peace is strength
Peace is lowly

Peace is rest
Peace is gentle

Peace is covenant
Peace is safety

Peace is gladness
Peace is being kept

Peace is unity
Peace is waiting

Scripture References:
1 Peter 3:11
Isaiah 43: 1-2, 4
Ephesians 4:3
Psalm 4:8
Isaiah 26:3
Psalm 85:8
1 Corinthians 14:33
John. 14:27

KINDNESS

Kindness is goodwill
Kindness is consideration
Kindness is mercifulness
Kindness is tender-heartedness

Kindness is compassion
Kindness is benevolence
Kindness is thoughtfulness
Kindness is generosity

Kindness is gentleness
Kindness is hospitality
Kindness is unselfishness
Kindness is warmth

Kindness is friendliness
Kindness is concern
Kindness is affection
Kindness is care

Scripture References:
Proverbs 11:17
Colossians 3:12
Ephesians 4:32
Luke 6:35
1 Corinthians 13:4-7

SELF-CONTROL

Self- control is self-discipline
Self-control is moderation

Self- control is self-restraint
Self- control is composure

Self- control is temperance
Self- control is will power

Self- control is coolness
Self- control is control

Self- control is mastery
Self- control is temperateness

Self- control is strength of will

Scripture References:
Proverbs 25:28
Galatians 5:22-23
2 Peter 1:5-7
1 Corinthians 9:24-27
1 Corinthians 9:27
1 Peter 4:7

GOODNESS

Goodness is compassion
Goodness is kindness

Goodness is virtue
Goodness is pleasantness

Goodness is graciousness
Goodness is valuable

Goodness is generosity
Goodness is satisfaction

Goodness is repentance

Scripture References:
Psalm 107:9
Romans 2: 4
Proverbs 2:20
Exodus 33: 19
1 Thessalonians 3:13
Psalm 65:11
John 10:11

GENTLENESS

Gentleness is kindness
Gentleness is consideration
Gentleness is amiability

Gentleness is tenderness
Gentleness is compassion
Gentleness is truth

Gentleness is caring
Gentleness is softness
Gentleness is moderation

Gentleness is calm
Gentleness is peaceful
Gentleness is tenderness

Gentleness is merciful
Gentleness is meekness
Gentleness is mild

Scripture References:
Titus 3:2
1 Peter 3:15
Psalm 18:35
2 Timothy 2:24-26
James 3:17
Galatians 6:1

PART SIX

Flow

A VIRGIN'S TALE

The story's been told
of how I got scold when they found out the gem I carried
I thank God for my husband who kept me strong
While everybody else thought I had done wrong

John the witness
Not the actual light
But sent to spread the word of the brightest light of the world

The disciples: a 12 men throng
They listened to His teachings
And followed Him day by day
Although they often got things wrong

A donkey's story
Carrying the King of glory
A manger worthy to receive the glory
Honour and praise brought to him by men so wise
Sought by a king

Adorned in rage
As he knew the real King would take his place

So the men from the East he encouraged
To give him the message

So he could offer up sacrilege
Shepherd boys left their sheep
Little did they know one day this Sheep would weep
As this shepherd was willing to keep
His pledge and his promise to leave the 99 saved
And sacrifice The Lamb for the soul of a lost sheep

That's pretty deep, right?
How deep is the Father's love for us?
That he would offer up a babe wrapped in swaddling cloth

For our anger, hurt, pain and wrong
And you could touch His face
By worshipping Him in song
Prayer, fasting and meditation goes a long way
So if you don't know Him like I do
Why not accept Him today?

He's waiting just like the world waited for The King
He's waiting for you to wait on Him!

Now for Him let your voices ring!
Hosanna in the Highest behold come Christ the King!
Your part in this great big story
Is to come to Christ
Tell others of His glory
Of how He died for you and me
Right on that tree
You see a life without Christ is a life without purpose
We need to get it together and make seeking God our focus
So when that great day comes
Around His throne
We will all be welcomed
So on that day
We won't hear the news
Stay away
Depart from me for I know you not

Scripture Reference:
For unto us a Child is born, Unto us a Son is given;
And the government will be upon His shoulder. And His name will be called Wonderful, Counselor, Mighty God, Everlasting Father, Prince of Peace.
Isaiah 9:6-7 (NKJV)

THE EARTH IS THE LORD'S

When the wind blows, Lord speak to me
When the trees move, whisper to me
When the birds sing, tweet me
When the rain falls,
shower me with your blessings

When the sun shines, keep me warm
As the world turns, keep me moving
Speak to me through your creation
I am alive and well.
In you I move,
breathe, live and have my being

As I close my eyes,
let me see you
As I open my ears,
let me hear you speak to me
As I open my mouth,
Lord speak through me
As I open my nose,
I want to smell your fragrance

As I breathe;
breathe new life into me
As I sing,
usher me into your presence
As I worship,
take me beyond the veil

As I praise,
place me in your tabernacle
As I pray,
let strongholds be broken
As I read,
may your truth come alive

As I meditate,
help me to look in retrospect at what you have done
As I thank you,
may you accept my worship
As I walk,
let me walk into your presence

As I run,
let me run to you and no other
As I kneel,
let me bring my all to you
As I lay down,
let me lay down in peace crowning You
Lord of all

Scripture Reference:
The heavens declare the glory of God, and the sky above proclaims his handiwork.
Psalm 19:1

WHEN MUSIC SPEAKS

When music speaks, people listen
Be it a nightingale
Or the latest beat

When music speaks, bodies shiver
People scream
Lips quiver

When music speaks,
Souls get saved
Love is found
You get lost in it

When music speaks,
The world unite
The times though challenging
Appears so bright

When music speaks,
There's fun and laughter
However, we fail to see the happy ever after

When music speaks,
People cry
For love lost
Some people die

When music speaks,
Soul ties are broken
There are things said
That would otherwise be unspoken

When music speaks,
People dance
There's another shot
Another chance

When music speaks,
You can live again
Embrace life
Challenge yourself

Embrace the music
When it speaks.

Scripture Reference:
My heart, O God, is steadfast, my heart is steadfast; I will sing and make music.
Psalm 57:8 (NIV)

THE COLOUR OF MY EMOTIONS

Sometimes green with bitterness
Sometimes blue with sadness
The colours of my feelings
Sometimes red with anger
Sometimes yellow with happiness
Sometimes pink with love
sometimes purple with joy and laughter
Sometimes white with peace
Sometimes black with dullness

I envision my feelings don't come to stay
Sometimes up
Sometimes down
Sometimes being pushed to the side
However, feelings are feelings
They are not necessarily real

The colours remind me of a rainbow
Of feelings based on emotions
Our feelings should not control our actions
as negative feelings will
result in negative impact

Scripture Reference:
A fool gives full vent to his spirit, but a wise man quietly holds it back.
Proverbs 29:11

Postscript

MUCH TO DO ABOUT NOTHING

Silent opportunities
Gone ever so wrong,
Why couldn't I be patient,
Why couldn't I stay strong?
The heart, so pure and rich as gold,
Has dried up.

So many invigorating thoughts,
Mindful insights are too imaginative
For anything to be actualised.
What's so wrong in my life?

Is God telling me that impurities
In the human form exist
Within which gets in the way
Of me realising and fulfilling
These hopes and dreams?

I am a long way from the perfect future;
Being settled and happy within.
Is there any peace in my life
Prolonged for continuous periods
Without discontentedness?

Inspiration lies deep
Within the surface far -fetched
And that's why once inspired
it's hard to let go or give in.
Once you've gotten that perfect lift, it's great.
Time to time, it's so difficult
To get by.

YOU HAVE MY HEART

Funny when you think you're
tough and got a heart of fire
that burns through everything.
Nothing cools you.
But then you start to realise
this life can go so far.

Also funny when you think
you've got a heart of stone
that no one can break;
very hard to hit.
But when Jesus' love
hits back at you,
your hearts crumbles.

Isn't it also funny when you think
you've got a heart of ice,
so cold that no warmth
and comfort can get close?
But then Jesus gets a hold of you
and suddenly your icebox melts.
You've got nothing to hold on to;
suddenly you're not so courageous.

FALLING IN LOVE WITH JESUS

Love in the instance
Putting up no resistance
To the change that has occurred
in my life
It's the way I live
It's the way I speak
That defies the movement
within my thoughts

My fears are relinquished
With clean hands
and a pure heart
and the power invested
in me by the Father,
I will prevail

Why?

Because I'm not a quitter;
never to give up
Spiritual upliftment
and sacrificial enlightening.
True passion and resilience
offer inner strength,
support, sculpture and guidance

GLOSSARY

ESV .... English Standard Version
NIV .... New International Version
KJV .... King James Version
GW .... God's Word Translation
HCSC .... Holy Christian Standard Bible
NKJV................ New King James Version

www.ingramcontent.com/pod-product-compliance
Lightning Source LLC
Chambersburg PA
CBHW021133300426
44113CB00006B/416